FOR US

DAILY DEVOTIONS FOR LENT & EASTER

TODD A. PEPERKORN

CONCORDIA PUBLISHING HOUSE • SAINT LOUIS

Copyright © 2026 Concordia Publishing House
3558 S. Jefferson Ave., St. Louis, MO 63118-3968
1-800-325-3040 • cph.org

All rights reserved. No part of this publication may be reproduced, stored in a retrieval system, or transmitted, in any form or by any means, electronic, mechanical, photocopying, recording, or otherwise, without the prior written permission of Concordia Publishing House.

Scripture quotations are from the ESV® Bible (The Holy Bible, English Standard Version®), copyright © 2001 by Crossway, a publishing ministry of Good News Publishers. Used by permission. All rights reserved.

Hymn texts with the abbreviation *LSB* are from *Lutheran Service Book* © 2006 Concordia Publishing House. All rights reserved.

Catechism quotation is taken from Luther's Small Catechism © 1986 Concordia Publishing House. All rights reserved.

The quotation from the Lutheran Confessions in this publication is from *Concordia: The Lutheran Confessions*, second edition © 2006 Concordia Publishing House. All rights reserved.

Manufactured in the United States of America

1 2 3 4 5 6 7 8 9 10   34 33 32 31 30 29 28 27 26 25

Ash Wednesday and the Days Following

ASH WEDNESDAY

Rending the Heart

Read Joel 2:12–19

"Yet even now," declares the Lord, "return to Me with all your heart, with fasting, with weeping, and with mourning; and rend your hearts and not your garments." (Joel 2:12–13)

God is not interested in what is on the outside. Keeping up appearances only goes so far, after all. What matters is what is on the inside.

But this internal focus does not come easily to us. We live in an age of appearances, of image, of only letting people see things as you want them to be seen, regardless of how they really are.

Our Lord has a better way for you and me.

His way, which we may call the way of the cross, is to recognize that we are dust, and to dust we shall return. We have fallen from the way of life, so the only path we know is the way of death.

In recognizing that we are dust, God calls us also to see and know that He does His best work with dust, with nothing, with the chaos of this world. He can and will make us new, after the image of His Son, Jesus Christ, our Lord. That is what it means to rend the heart.

Heavenly Father, we know You do everything for us and our good. Teach us to rend our hearts so that You may make us new by Your Holy Spirit. In Jesus' name. Amen.

THURSDAY AFTER ASH WEDNESDAY

Becoming the Righteousness of God

Read 2 Corinthians 5:20–6:10

For our sake, He made Him to be sin who knew no sin, so that in Him we might become the righteousness of God. (2 Corinthians 5:21)

Today's Scripture is both one of the easiest and the hardest verses in the Bible to understand. It is easy because the concept of the Great Exchange is easy. Jesus took what is bad in us and gave us all that is good in Himself. Simple. It is a straight-up trade, a sweet swap, and a deal like no other.

And yet it is the hardest verse in the Bible to understand. How can the eternal Son of God, holy and perfect in every way, *become sin* for us? How can He, who is righteous, holy, pure, and perfect, take on our filth, sorrow, hardship, pain, and death? It is incomprehensible. We cannot understand it, and we never will.

The answer lies in the word *incarnation*. The word means "to become flesh." The mystery is that by taking on our flesh and blood, Christ takes on our very humanity. As we confess in the creed, "Who for us men and for our salvation . . . was made man." This is the mystery of the ages for us.

Jesus, thank You for taking on our sin for us so that we may become the righteousness of God. Amen.

FRIDAY AFTER ASH WEDNESDAY

The Treasure

Read Matthew 6:1–6, 16–21

For where your treasure is, there your heart will be also. (Matthew 6:21)

This verse always seems backward to me. Shouldn't it work the other way—where your heart is, there your treasure will be also? I mean, shouldn't our heart be what is driving things here?

No, Jesus has it right. Our external actions point to the internal reality. If we invest our earthly treasures in things that will rust and fade away, then we are saying earthly things are what are truly important.

The ancients might have called earthly things "the passions." We might say our true desires. Consider the words from the Individual Confession and Absolution of sins in *Lutheran Service Book*: "My thoughts and desires have been soiled by sin" (p. 292).

Left to our own devices, our hearts will often lead us astray. But there is good news. Thank God that Jesus has given you a new heart! We pray in Psalm 51 that God would create in us a new heart, and He does so in Holy Baptism.

Because of your new heart, every day is a new beginning. Every day we drown the old, sinful desires and rise again to serve Him. That is why Jesus is our true, priceless treasure. He is the only one who can make all things news.

Jesus, You are our priceless treasure. Help us ever to keep our eyes fixed on You. Amen.

SATURDAY AFTER ASH WEDNESDAY

Restored

Read Psalm 51:1–13 (14–19)

Restore to me the joy of Your salvation, and uphold me with a willing spirit. (Psalm 51:12)

It is incredible how quickly we can forget the joy of salvation. A bad day at work or school, a flare-up of anger—Satan loves nothing more than to rob the Christian of true joy in Christ.

It has been said that joy is happiness tempered by sorrow. Sorrow over sin leads, by God's Word and Spirit, to true joy in the salvation won for us by Jesus Christ.

We experience sadness and sorrow. We suffer because of our sins, but we also suffer because of the sins of others. In restoring the joy of your salvation, God takes all that sadness and suffering and leaves it at the foot of the cross. There, Jesus takes it into Himself. And in its place, He puts joy—true joy—in Him.

God gives you a willing spirit for this daily dying and rising, this continual restoration of joy. This spirit comes only by faith. It is a spirit that says amen to everything God has in store for you, even if you do not know the way. He will give this spirit to you.

Lord, break down the stubbornness of my heart and give me a willing spirit, so I may receive the holy joy that only comes from You. In Jesus' name. Amen.

Lent
Week One

FIRST SUNDAY IN LENT

By the Word Alone

Read Matthew 4:1–4

It is written, "Man shall not live by bread alone, but by every word that comes from the mouth of God." (Matthew 4:4)

Shortly after Jesus' time on earth, the Roman poet Juvenal criticized Roman citizens for only wanting to be fed and entertained. Bread and circuses, he called it. You would think he was talking about today.

It certainly seems like our desire to think short-term, our want to satisfy our basest desires, is hardwired into our sinful flesh. Money, time, people—you name it. It all comes down to bread and circuses for the fallen sons and daughters of Adam.

Maybe Juvenal had heard of Jesus' temptation in the wilderness. Satan tempted Jesus by commanding Him to turn stone into bread. While this may not seem like a big deal on the surface, it is indeed quite a big deal. Satan was asking Jesus to use His divine powers not to save us but to satisfy Himself. Satan tempts us with our human desires also, every day. So much so that we often forget how self-centered we truly are.

But it is not so with Jesus. In Christ, we glimpse a picture of humanity as God intended it. Jesus does not eat for Himself. His bread is not the bread that comes and is gone in a flash. His bread, which He gives to you and me, is His body and blood. Now that is real food for us.

Lord, teach me to live by Your Word alone. In Jesus' name. Amen.

MONDAY, LENT 1

Look for the Helpers

Read Matthew 4:5–11

Then the devil left Him, and behold, angels came and were ministering to Him. (Matthew 4:11)

There is something incredibly comforting in knowing that Jesus had angels who ministered to Him after His temptation in the wilderness. Jesus Christ, the Son of God and Son of Mary, has people— angels, in this case—to care for Him in His hour of need.

The word translated as *minister* here simply means "to serve" in English. The angels served Him. Served Him what? Food and drink? A place to rest His weary head? Our text does not say, but those make the most sense. Jesus had undergone a great trial, fasting forty days and nights, and He was hungry and needed a Sabbath, a rest from His weariness.

When you have undergone a great trial, when you have done battle with Satan and with your flesh, how are you cared for? Sometimes our heavenly Father will send angels into our midst, but more often today, He sends earthly servants to care for us. These messengers may be pastors, who preach to you, or family or friends, who share God's Word with you. And He may send other helpers to care for you, body and soul.

As you undergo temptations and trials in life, remember what Mr. Rodgers said many years ago and look for the helpers.

Heavenly Father, send Your holy angels to watch over and keep me, just like they did for Your Son, Jesus. In His name. Amen.

TUESDAY, LENT 1

Enmity

Read Genesis 3:1–21

> I will put enmity between you and the woman,
> and between your offspring and her offspring;
> He shall bruise your head, and you shall bruise
> His heel. (Genesis 3:15)

The enemy of my enemy is my friend, as the saying goes. But in this case, it is way more complicated than that. In Genesis 3:15, we have what is known as the protoevangelium, or the first Gospel in the Scriptures.

Notice that God is addressing the serpent, not Adam and Eve. In cursing the serpent, Satan, God blesses the whole human race.

Jesus Christ, the promised Seed from the woman, battles Satan himself. Jesus conquers sin, death, and the power of the devil by shedding His blood on the cross for us. In doing this, He "bruises the head" of Satan, even while it costs Him His own life.

The enemy of my enemy *is* my friend. Jesus Christ, the friend of sinners, battles sin, death, and the power of the devil for you and me. His obedience is His weapon, His life is the cost, and our salvation is the prize. Thank God that He is a God for us!

Jesus, help me to see that You conquered Satan by being obedient to death, even death on the cross. Amen.

WEDNESDAY, LENT 1

By His Son

Read Hebrews 1:1–14

Long ago, at many times and in many ways, God spoke to our fathers by the prophets, but in these last days He has spoken to us by His Son. (Hebrews 1:1–2)

God speaks through the Word. That is who He is. That is how He communicates to us. Any conversation with God apart from His external Word is uncertain and suspect. Luther puts it this way: "In issues relating to the spoken, outward Word, we must firmly hold that God grants His Spirit or grace to no one except through or with the preceding outward Word [Galatians 3:2, 5]" (Smalcald Articles, Part 3, Article 8, paragraph 3).

First, He spoke through the prophets of old. But now, He speaks to us through Jesus Christ, His Son, our Lord.

Why is this comforting? It is comforting because we know that God is merciful, loves us with an everlasting love, and wants nothing for us but good. That is what His Word teaches. Even when He speaks Law, it is because He loves us.

Do not let anything or anyone—not Satan, not death, not even your own heart—pull you away from the pure comfort that only comes from Jesus Christ. "My flesh and my heart may fail, but God is the strength of my heart and my portion forever" (Psalm 73:26).

Jesus, continue to speak to us through Your Holy Word. Amen.

THURSDAY, LENT 1

Saved by Obedience

Read Romans 5:12–19

For as by the one man's disobedience the many were made sinners, so by the one man's obedience the many will be made righteous. (Romans 5:19)

"That's not fair!" You can almost hear the expression from children on the playground or disgruntled coworkers. We are obsessed with fairness, as long as such fairness benefits us in the end.

That is why this passage, and the whole teaching on sin, is sometimes hard for us to receive. Why should I be responsible for what one of my ancestors did thousands of years ago? It does not make sense; it isn't fair.

Yet it is true. We sometimes will use the phrase *original sin* to talk about this sin. I tend to like the expression *inherited sin* more. We inherit our sinfulness in the same way we inherit hair color, height, skin tone, and other genetic traits. I have inherited this, so it is part of the package of being human.

But that is also why this is a gift and a mystery. Jesus inherited all of our humanity, except for the sin, through His mother, Mary. He is the new Adam, untainted by the garden and the fall. Through His obedience, we all become righteous and holy before God.

Now that is a gift to be reckoned with.

Father, thank You for sending Your Son so I might live in Him. In Jesus' name. Amen.

FRIDAY, LENT 1

Wasted Away

Read Psalm 32:1–4

For when I kept silent, my bones wasted away through my groaning all day long. For day and night Your hand was heavy upon me; my strength was dried up as by the heat of summer. (Psalm 32:3–4)

Psalm 32 is one of the penitential psalms. We know that God speaks to us through His Word, and sometimes, that Word gives voice to the darkest corners of the heart.

That is what we have in Psalm 32. In this psalm, King David rejoices in the gift of forgiveness in God's voice and describes what it is like when we do not receive that forgiveness.

In some ways, it is easy to think of sin as an idea, a concept, or even an attitude. There is truth to all of those in some ways. But sin is much more insidious, much more dangerous than that. It is a disease, an infection of the soul. It eats at us, corrupts us, and wants nothing more than to destroy us.

David rightly shows how sin can be physically painful. His body is affected by this inherited sin, and so are ours.

But remember how he begins: "Blessed is the one whose transgression is forgiven, whose sin is covered" (Psalm 32:1). That forgiveness is the final gift for us.

Jesus, even though I waste away, be my stronghold, strengthen me, and feed me with the bread of Your Word. Amen.

SATURDAY, LENT 1

Hiding in God

Read Psalm 32:5–7

You are a hiding place for me; You preserve me from trouble; You surround me with shouts of deliverance. (Psalm 32:7)

Yesterday, we heard what happens when we hide *from God*. Today, we listen to what it means to hide *in God*.

By covering our sins, God hides us in Himself. We become a part of His holy family once again, and because of this, we need not fear sin, death, or the devil himself.

Whom or what do you fear? Our heavenly Father longs to protect you from it all: big or small, serious or slight. That is His nature. That is His identity. And because Christ took on our human nature, He experienced life on earth for you, yet He was without sin.

In a culture riddled with anxiety over everything, big or little, there is great comfort in knowing that Christ, who is our true light, enlightens the darkness of our hearts by His gracious visitation.

Everyone needs to have a place of safety, a hideaway where no one can get to you and where you are free from worry, harm, and sorrow. That hiding place is God Himself. Be wrapped up in His mercy, for He will guard you from all harm.

Father, teach me to hide in You, and help me to see that Your strong right hand is always guarding me. In Jesus' name. Amen.

Lent
Week Two

SECOND SUNDAY IN LENT

A Command and a Promise

Read Genesis 12:1–3

Now the Lord said to Abram, "Go from your country and your kindred and your father's house to the land that I will show you." (Genesis 12:1)

God commanded Abram (later Abraham) to go from his country and people to a land God would show him. That is quite an ask, isn't it? Would you take such a journey, sight unseen?

In many respects, this is the walk of the Christian life. We know the promises; we hear them over and over again. But we do not know *exactly* how they will work out. Some parts of the journey are easy and joyful, but others are dark and lonely, and we cannot see the ending.

When God asks something of us that is outside what we know, remember first that Christ is with us all the way and second that God will not abandon us because things are hard or dark. Far from it! I would argue that God does His best work when things are darkest. Think of Lazarus, Elijah, the prophets of Baal, or even Jesus' death on the cross. It would be fair to say that seeing the ending in these cases was impossible. God's merciful presence isn't a guess, though. It is something we can cling to by faith.

Lord, help us when we don't know the way but only that You guide us. In Jesus' name. Amen.

MONDAY, LENT 2

To Your Offspring

Read Genesis 12:4–9

Then the Lord appeared to Abram and said, "To your offspring I will give this land." (Genesis 12:7)

It is hard for us to fully understand the relationship of the people of Abram (Abraham) to the land. This relationship was promised to them by God Himself in Genesis and later to Moses and the Israelites in Deuteronomy. God's promise to be with and care for His people always has a concreteness. His people have an identity, a place, a land to call their own.

His promise to us is, in many ways, the same. We are the spiritual offspring, or heirs, of Abraham. God made this covenant, this promise, to Abraham, and that promise was fulfilled for us in Christ.

This promise means that you have a place. You have an altar, a table from which Jesus' very body and blood are given to you for the forgiveness of your sins.

What's more, you have the promise of new heavens and a new earth and that you will be forever in the new Jerusalem, the city not built with hands. All these promises are fulfilled in Jesus, and you will live in Him forevermore.

Jesus, help me to see myself in God's promises to His people. Amen.

TUESDAY, LENT 2

The Lord Is Your Keeper

Read Psalm 121

> The Lord will keep you from all evil; He will keep your life. The Lord will keep your going out and your coming in from this time forth and forevermore. (Psalm 121:7–8)

In this entire psalm, only one sentence has us (or David) as the subject: "I lift up my eyes to the hills" (v. 1). All David, and we, can do is watch and see the mighty works of God unfold. In some ways, it is reminiscent of Moses telling Israel that they need only to be silent and watch as God protects them from Pharaoh (see Exodus 14:13–14).

And what did God do for David and all Israel? He didn't let their foot be moved. He kept them from all evil; He didn't sleep. He was their shade. He kept their lives, their comings and goings, every step of the way.

Not even the sun or moon could strike them (v. 6). They were completely and utterly safe in God's keeping.

So are you. As His holy child, you are safe and secure in the holy ark of Christendom, resting in the palm of His hands. No matter what may come, God will be with you. Not even death can keep God and His love in Jesus Christ from you. You are kept in God.

Lord, keep my comings and goings safe in Your arms all the days of my life. In Jesus' name. Amen.

WEDNESDAY, LENT 2

Pleased

Read Mark 1:9–13

And a voice came from heaven, "You are My beloved Son; with You I am well pleased." (Mark 1:11)

Nearly everyone appreciates the praise of their father or mother. Receiving and enjoying praise and encouragement is a part of what makes us human. So hearing the Father say that He is pleased with His Son is a pretty normal thing to happen, isn't it?

Yes, but there is more going on than meets the eye. Jesus is not simply a son; He is *the* Son, the only-begotten one, who takes away the sin of the world. His Baptism is not for Himself but for us, as the hymn attests:

> For us baptized, for us He bore
> His holy fast and hungered sore;
> For us temptation sharp He knew;
> For us the tempter overthrew. (*LSB* 544:3)

Jesus' Baptism was the public beginning of His ministry on earth, and it propelled Him forward through the temptation of Satan and back again. Like Israel wandering in the wilderness for forty years, Jesus wandered for forty days. Only where Israel failed did Jesus succeed in fighting off temptation. In doing this, Jesus overthrew the tempter.

That is where you come in. Christ was baptized for us, so His victory over temptation is *your* victory. Rejoice in the victory and remember who you are in your Baptism!

Lord, keep us in our Baptism so that we may find our rest and hope in You. In Jesus' name. Amen.

THURSDAY, LENT 2

Counted as Righteousness

Read Romans 4:1–8

To the one who does not work but believes in Him who justifies the ungodly, his faith is counted as righteousness. (Romans 4:5)

St. Paul loves to use Abraham as a great example of justification by faith. In Romans 4, Paul argues that if works save us, it is simply like a paid wage for what someone is owed. But we cannot be saved by works because we could never work enough to pay off our debt.

On the other hand, Abraham lived according to the promise of faith. He trusted that when the Lord makes a promise, He will keep it. God promised Abraham that He would receive a new land. Eventually, Abraham was promised his descendants (offspring) would number like the stars in the sky or the sands on the seashore.

Now, God does not promise you land, at least not in an earthly way. But He does promise you and me that we will be a part of the new creation, that He will make new heavens and a new earth, and even that He will make all things new.

Does that bring you comfort? It should. God promises to make all things new. And because you are justified by grace through faith, you, too, will receive the promised inheritance.

Jesus, thank You for grafting me into Your family so that I may receive the promised inheritance in You. Amen.

FRIDAY, LENT 2

The Righteousness of Faith

Read Romans 4:13–17

For the promise to Abraham and his offspring that he would be heir of the world did not come through the law but through the righteousness of faith. (Romans 4:13)

All of the great promises of God given to him come through the "righteousness of faith." But what is faith?

Faith, trust, belief—they all mean the same thing. They mean relying on someone or something to do something. I can have faith or trust in a person or a thing. I could trust, for example, that the roof over my head will not collapse. My trust in this is based on my observations to some extent, but ultimately, I have to trust that the people who built the house did what they said in building it correctly.

When we talk about faith in the promises of God, we are saying that we rely on what God says in His Word. God says that I am justified by grace through faith, apart from the deeds of the Law. I trust that it is true. This faith is not based on evidence that I can see but on what He has told me in His Word. He does this for us so that we may live in Him.

Lord God, give me faith to trust in Your Word of promise. In Jesus' name. Amen.

SATURDAY, LENT 2

In This Way

Read John 3:1–17

For God so loved the world, that He gave His only Son, that whoever believes in Him should not perish but have eternal life. (John 3:16)

For such a simple verse, this is quite tricky to translate! In idiomatic English, we would say something like this: "For God loved the world in this way, that He gave His only-begotten Son, so that whoever believes in Him should not perish but have eternal life." The question in our text is not about *how much* God loves us; that is impossible to answer or measure. The question is, really, how God *shows* His love to us.

In other words, God sent His Son for us. That is how He shows us His love. He is present in the Word made flesh, and that same Word is the once-for-all sacrifice to pay the price for our sins.

God's love is clear, demonstrable, and exactly what we need to live. God's love is also what ties Jesus' death to our Baptism. When we are baptized, we are baptized into Jesus' death and resurrection. His death and life are now ours by faith.

What a gift! What a treasure! What a Savior! And it is all for us.

Jesus, thank You for showing me how God loves me through You. Amen.

Lent
Week Three

THIRD SUNDAY IN LENT

Water for Us

Read Exodus 17:1–7

Behold, I will stand before you there on the rock at Horeb, and you shall strike the rock, and water shall come out of it, and the people will drink. (Exodus 17:6)

Pharaoh was defeated. The people of Israel were in the wilderness but safe from the hands of their enemies. It was the perfect time to complain about the water.

How many times have we done the same? Delivered from sin, death, and the power of the devil, and yet somehow, we end up complaining about the accommodations and food at our divine homecoming.

God does not strike us down, though. He does not end us as we deserve. And we, like Israel, do deserve nothing but death and punishment.

This is a sign of God's great mercy. Even though we do not deserve it, He continues to give us Christ. St. Paul wrote about the Israelites, "For they drank from the spiritual Rock that followed them, and the Rock was Christ" (1 Corinthians 10:4).

God cares for us, body and soul. Even His care for our physical needs points to how He ultimately fulfills our every need in Jesus.

When you complain, and we all do, bring your complaints to Jesus. He is the only one who can make things right in this world and the next.

Jesus, teach us to be grateful for all You do for us. Amen.

MONDAY, LENT 3

Kneeling Before God

Read Psalm 95:1–9

Oh come, let us worship and bow down; let us kneel before the Lord, our Maker! (Psalm 95:6)

Psalm 95 is best known among us for the canticle in Matins: "Oh come, let us sing to the Lord" (v. 1). This verse is a part of that great call to worship.

One of the common traits of worship in the Old Testament is that there is always a connection between what we *do* and what we *believe*. Even the word for *worship* in Hebrew means "to bow down." Thus, there is a physicality to worship that we sometimes forget. Worship doesn't just mean thinking "Jesus thoughts" in our heads. God wants all of us, not just our minds. And I want to worship God in spirit and body, just like the apostles did!

An important thing to remember here is that we do not *have* to do certain ceremonies to curry God's favor. It is just the opposite. We kneel before God because He alone is worthy of praise. We kneel because we are not worthy to be in His holy presence. And we kneel because He is the God who does everything for us and gives us Himself through His Word and Spirit.

The next time you go to church, reflect on standing, sitting, and kneeling. They each have a place in Lutheran worship; these actions are a fruit of faith and for our good.

Lord, teach us to worship You in everything we say and do. In Jesus' name. Amen.

TUESDAY, LENT 3

Peace

Read Romans 5:1–8

Therefore, since we have been justified by faith, we have peace with God through our Lord Jesus Christ. (Romans 5:1)

Peace with God is the result of our justification by faith. No justification, no peace. This simple but profound reality is what St. Paul unveils for us in chapter 5 of Romans. Because we have been justified and declared righteous in His sight, all these things are now ours: grace, suffering, endurance, character, and hope. All of these flow from peace with God.

We often try to do this backward. If I can make things right with God, then He will forgive me. If I do certain things, then God will receive me into His holy family once again. This is precisely why Paul continues by saying, "For while we were still weak, at the right time Christ died for the ungodly" (Romans 5:6). Christ died for the weak, the lost, and those who are dead in trespasses and sin. That means you and me. We receive peace from God as a gift, through the sacrifice of Jesus on the cross.

But what does peace with God mean? It means you need never be afraid. It means you know who you are as a baptized child of God. It means you do not have to wonder what God thinks about you. Justified by faith, you have true peace with God.

Heavenly Father, teach us to live in the peace only You can give us through Your Son, Jesus Christ, our Lord. In His name. Amen.

WEDNESDAY, LENT 3

Praying in the Dark

Read Mark 1:35–39

And rising very early in the morning, while it was still dark, He departed and went out to a desolate place, and there He prayed. (Mark 1:35)

Why pray in the darkness? Jesus Christ is the light of the world, as we pray in our evening prayer liturgy. Yet here He is praying early in the morning, in the darkness and desolation of the wilderness.

He prays in the darkness because that is where He finds us. Lost in the darkness and the shadow of death, our lives, at times, are more like desolate wilderness than green pastures. Because of sin, our lives can become wild and chaotic, and we may be uncertain of what comes next or why.

So Jesus prays for us, especially in the darkness and desolation of our lives. His taking on of our flesh and blood means that He enters into the darkness, your darkness, because that is where He finds you. He prays for you and with you, knowing that you will not get yourself out of the mess and muck on your own.

Jesus does not stop there, though. He does not sit by as you suffer. He takes the darkness, even death, into Himself. While you may live and struggle in darkness now, the dawn is coming. Jesus will be there with you.

Lord, teach us to pray even when surrounded by darkness. In Jesus' name. Amen.

THURSDAY, LENT 3

The Fountain

Read John 4:5–15

Whoever drinks of the water that I will give
him will never be thirsty again. (John 4:14)

Jesus sat down by the well of Jacob. He was weary from traveling. While sitting, He asked a woman for a drink of water. This meeting at the well seems innocent enough to us, but in Jesus' day, this was a major faux pas. The Samaritan woman was an adulterer, married five times. She was not the kind of person you would expect the Lord of Life to associate with.

But you would be wrong. Jesus came to save the weak, the ungodly, the ones dead in trespasses and sins. Sometimes, we are so dead that we don't even know it, like the woman in our text.

Jesus offered her the water that springs up to eternal life. In the ancient world, water was often associated with the beginnings of life, so Jesus giving her water that leads to eternal life is like Him saying, "The teaching that I will give you will not just be for now—it will be for all eternity."

It would take time for her to get the whole picture, but the water was coming. Soon, a flood of mercy would be upon her.

Lord, teach me to drink from Your teachings so that I may never thirst for the life only You can give. In Jesus' name. Amen.

FRIDAY, LENT 3

Speaking the Truth in Love

Read John 4:16–20

Jesus said to her, "Go, call your husband, and come here." The woman answered Him, "I have no husband." (John 4:16–17)

What the woman said was both true and untrue. It was true that she had no husband because the man she was with was not her husband, and she had been married five times before.

Why does Jesus say this to her? Isn't it mean of Him to point out the darkness of her life? Jesus is using the Law here surgically. He points out her sin so that she can see who she is according to the Law of God: a sinner. The Word of God is sharper than any two-edged sword, and when the Law cuts, it cuts deep.

There are times in our lives when the Law cuts us. It may be a Scripture verse that hits hard. It may be a sermon or even a tough conversation with a friend. But the Law does its work, and sometimes we are unhappy about it.

Ultimately, there are only two responses to the Law: We either repent of our sin, or we rebel against the one who made the Law in the first place. Jesus calls her to repentance here, just like He calls you and me. It is a hard word, but it is not the last word.

Lord, teach me to receive Your Word of truth with repentance and faith. In Jesus' name. Amen.

SATURDAY, LENT 3

In Spirit and in Truth

Read John 4:21–26

God is spirit, and those who worship Him must worship in spirit and truth. (John 4:24)

Spirit is certainly one of the most confusing words in the English language. We use *spirit* to refer to physical versus nonphysical ("mind, body, and spirit"). We also use *spirit* to talk about attitude ("That's the spirit!"). We even use it to say that someone is like God ("They are spiritual."). So, how does Jesus use it here?

God is Spirit and is not bound by physical location. St. Augustine puts it this way:

> Both the Father is a spirit and the Son is a spirit, and the Father is holy and the Son is holy. ... [The Holy Spirit] is referred both to the Father and to the Son, because the Holy Spirit is the Spirit both of the Father and of the Son.[1]

Worship ultimately means receiving God according to His word and promise by faith. It isn't ultimately about the location, but that the Word is present. As Jesus says elsewhere, "Where two or three are gathered in My name, there I am in the midst of them" (Matthew 18:20).

Lord, give me Your Holy Spirit by Your Word, so that I may worship in Spirit and in truth. In Jesus' name. Amen.

---

[1] Augustine, *On the Holy Trinity,* 5.9.1 (*NPNF* 1/3:93), as quoted in Edward A. Engelbrecht, ed., *The Lutheran Study Bible* (Concordia Publishing House, 2009), 1787.

Lent
Week Four

FOURTH SUNDAY IN LENT

Saved from Ourselves

Read Isaiah 42:14–21

They are turned back and utterly put to shame, who trust in carved idols, who say to metal images, "You are our gods." (Isaiah 42:17)

Isaiah 42 is a painful description of what the idol worshipers in Isaiah's day were like. The people of Israel had forgotten their God, the one who had saved them from the hand of Pharaoh. They had turned to the practices of their neighbors in the land, to the worship of metal and stone and carved images meant to house the so-called gods of the people.

In one way, this sounds hard for us to understand. I mean, who worships a rock or a piece of metal? It sounds primitive and quaint, like something before our time.

But is it really so hard to believe that people worshiped the creation rather than the Creator? Our worship of created things may not be as crass as the people of Israel's so many years ago, but it is no less idolatry. We have found ways to put phones or houses, clothes or computers, or whatever it might be before our heavenly Father.

Thank God Jesus came not in a carved image or metal but in flesh and blood like you and me. He came for us so that we might be saved, even from ourselves.

Lord, teach us to ever trust in You alone. In Jesus' name. Amen.

MONDAY, LENT 4

Pay Attention!

Read Psalm 142

Attend to my cry, for I am brought very low!
Deliver me from my persecutors, for they are
too strong for me! (Psalm 142:6)

Listen to me! You can almost feel the desperation in David's words. He is hiding in a cave, trying to keep away from Saul and those who would persecute him. And he pours out his heart to God.

This psalm is called a lament, or complaint. When we suffer and undergo trials, it is easy to feel isolated. I am alone, and no one knows or cares what is happening. This is why David cries out, "Attend to my cry!" It is as if he is saying, "Pay attention, Lord! I need you! Listen to me!" There is something to be said about voicing your fears, even if the fear is that no one is listening. Even when David laments, he does so from the position of faith. Why talk to God at all if you do not trust in Him?

In a psalm of lament like this one, we see that God longs to hear our prayers, wants to hear our complaints, and, most importantly, will answer us. This isn't simply a case of active listening on God's part; He hears, and He will answer.

Cry out to God. Let Him have it! He can take it.

Lord, hear my pleas for mercy and give me Your grace. In Jesus' name. Amen.

TUESDAY, LENT 4

Light in the Lord

Read Ephesians 5:8–14

For at one time you were darkness, but now you are light in the Lord. Walk as children of light. (Ephesians 5:8)

Sometimes in the Bible, you will see a metaphor or an analogy that cuts to the heart. "At one time you were darkness," Paul says. Note that he does not say that you were *in* darkness or that you were *consumed by* darkness. No, Paul says that you *were darkness* itself.

Sometimes when we talk about sin, we talk about being caught in a trespass or being trapped. This is undoubtedly true, but Paul goes a step further. He points at you and says that you *are* the darkness. Ouch.

But just as he says you *were* the darkness, in the same way, he says that now you *are* light in the Lord. Darkness: past tense. Light: present tense. The darkness no longer defines you; it no longer shapes you. The darkness has been washed away, and now you are light in the Lord. You are baptized into Christ, and you are en*light*ened by Him.

Paul then says to walk as children of the light. In other words, Paul tells us to act like Christians. We may still do dark (sinful) things, but they should not define who we are or draw us away from God. Be who you are as His child of light!

Jesus, enlighten us with Your Word so we may be Your children. Amen.

WEDNESDAY, LENT 4

The Legion Is Gone

Read Mark 5:1–13

And when Jesus had stepped out of the boat, immediately there met Him out of the tombs a man with an unclean spirit. (Mark 5:2)

Everywhere Jesus went, He was confronted with sin, death, and the power of the devil. Even here, on the eastern shore of the Sea of Galilee, they came for Him. The demon's name was Legion, the name for a unit of about six thousand men in the Roman army. This man had been tormented horribly. No one could help him.

No one but Jesus.

Jesus cast the demons out of the man using only His words, commanding, "Come out of the man, you unclean spirit!" This only happened by God's authority and the power of His Word. Jesus is the Word made flesh, so His words mean what they say; His words have power over all evil.

When Jesus takes on sin, death, and the devil, He does so for us. Your struggles against sin and death and Satan happen every day. Sometimes they are more obvious, but other times they are sneaky and subtle, hiding until the opportune time to come out.

When Jesus was confronted with this poor man, He took care of him immediately. He cast out the demons. So it is with you. Jesus forgives your sins and draws you to Himself—now, not later. His desire for you takes a back seat to no one.

Jesus, save me when I fall under attack. Amen.

THURSDAY, LENT 4

The Works of God for Us

Read John 9:1–7

Jesus answered, "It was not that this man sinned, or his parents, but that the works of God might be displayed in him." (John 9:3)

The man had been blind from birth. All he had ever known was darkness. In Jesus' day, if someone had an illness or genetic disease, the assumption was that somehow it was the direct result of sin. So the Pharisees asked Jesus if this man had sinned or if his parents had.

Jesus turned the whole thing upside down and said it wasn't about sin at all, but so the "works of God" might be displayed or shown. It turns out there is more going on than meets the eye.

Death is the result of sin. Even if we cannot point to cause and effect, we still know that death is in the world because of sin. Anytime disaster strikes, whether it is an individual illness or a huge calamity, this is always a cause for us to repent of our sin and look to God for grace.

What Jesus does here is point to the fact that God does not *end* with judgment. Not for this man, and not for us. While bad things happen in the world because of our sin, that is not the end of the story. Christ died and rose for the forgiveness of our sins so that our story might end with Him in heaven. He gives this salvation to you and me by faith. That is God's work.

Lord, work faith in me so I may always trust in Your mighty works of salvation. In Jesus' name. Amen.

FRIDAY, LENT 4

More than a Prophet

Read John 9:13–17

So they said again to the blind man, "What do you say about Him, since He has opened your eyes?" He said, "He is a prophet." (John 9:17)

The Pharisees are baffled by Jesus and this formerly blind man. Jesus acts like a rabbi but heals on the Sabbath. If he's breaking their rules for the Sabbath, He can't be from God, can He? And yet, where else could this ability to truly heal come from?

The man answered that Jesus is a prophet. Like the healing prophets of old, Jesus seemed to bring the Pharisees back to another time, when God was somehow closer to them and more real, perhaps.

It is true, of course, that Jesus is a prophet. He is *the* Prophet, the One promised, who would be like Moses. But He is not just a prophet who speaks God's Word to the people. No, Jesus is the very Word made flesh. He is the new Israel, the greater Moses, the one to come who would make all things right.

Sometimes, like the Pharisees in our text, we do not understand how God is at work. Ultimately, it may be a mystery that will not be revealed until the Last Day. That is okay. Christ has revealed Himself to us as the only begotten Son of God. That is miraculous enough.

Jesus, open my heart to know You as You reveal Yourself in the Scriptures. Amen.

SATURDAY, LENT 4

Seeing Truly

Read John 9:34–39

Jesus said, "For judgment I came into this world, that those who do not see may see, and those who see may become blind." (John 9:39)

The theology of the cross is at the very heart of Lutheran theology. Jesus Himself expresses it in this section of John's Gospel.

Jesus talks to this formerly blind man, who can now see. He uses the theology of the cross as a way to teach us how to accept what we cannot know or do before God can reveal His good and gracious will to us. We put it this way in the Small Catechism:

> I believe that I cannot by my own reason or strength believe in Jesus Christ, my Lord, or come to Him; but the Holy Spirit has called me by the Gospel, enlightened me with His gifts, sanctified and kept me in the true faith. (Luther's explanation of the Third Article of the Nicene Creed)

I believe that I cannot believe. Once I recognize that, God gets to work with His Gospel, forgiving sins and bringing new life. The blind can now see because God has revealed the truth.

But the Scriptures remain a closed book for those who think they have it all together. Until you know you are blind, you cannot begin to see what Jesus has to give to you.

Lord, teach me to trust in Your holy will, as You have revealed it to us in the Scriptures. In Jesus' name. Amen.

Lent Week Five

FIFTH SUNDAY IN LENT

Dry Bones

Read Ezekiel 37:1–14

> And you shall know that I am the Lord, when I open your graves, and raise you from your graves, O My people. (Ezekiel 37:13)

Ezekiel 37 tells of the prophet's vision while he is in the Spirit. God shows him how the people of Israel are dead. They are dry bones with no life left in them. Ezekiel prophesies to them, and the Lord breathes life into them.

Can you imagine the scene, a whole valley of death? That is what we are apart from the breath of life, which only God can give.

Jesus' death for the sins of the world means that we can have life, real life, and have it abundantly. God will breathe new life into your dry bones and mine. We sing about this in the hymn "God's Own Child, I Gladly Say It":

> Death, you cannot end my gladness:
> I am baptized into Christ!
> When I die, I leave all sadness
> To inherit paradise!
> Though I lie in dust and ashes
> Faith's assurance brightly flashes:
> Baptism has the strength divine
> To make life immortal mine. (*LSB* 594:3)

By faith, we now see things through God's eyes. While things may be hard, the trials may continue, and we may be surrounded by death on every side, God brings new life. Always.

Lord, breathe new life into these dry bones so that I may live according to Your Word. In Jesus' name. Amen.

MONDAY, LENT 5

Steadfast Love

Read Psalm 130

O Israel, hope in the Lord! For with the Lord there is steadfast love, and with him is plentiful redemption. (Psalm 130:7)

The psalm begins with the words "Out of the depths I cry to you, O Lord." If you are like me, there are times when crying from the depths is exactly what you do.

In this psalm, the cry is about sin. We cry out because our guilt overwhelms us, engulfs us, and drowns us with its weight. The consequences of our sin may overwhelm us, but sin flows from one corrupt root.

David cries out of the depths, we cry out of the depths, and so does Jesus, who prays this prayer with you and for you. He takes your sin into Himself and now bears that sin for you to death itself.

But the psalmist does not just stay there. We are not just crushed and left to our own devices. Hope means looking forward to what God is going to do. Do you believe God loves you and wants you to be with Him forever? Why?

God's steadfast love means that He always keeps His promises. He continues to keep the covenant He made. His redemption is always full, always plenteous. There is more than enough to go around.

You may be in the depths, but God will lift you up. It is who He is.

Lord, pull us out of the depths so we may ever praise You. In Jesus' name. Amen.

TUESDAY, LENT 5

No Condemnation

Read Romans 8:1–11

There is therefore now no condemnation for those who are in Christ Jesus. (Romans 8:1)

To be in Christ is to be baptized into His death. Because you have been baptized into Him, your fate and future are bound to His. He dies, you die. He rises from the dead, and you rise from the dead.

Christ, through the power of the Holy Spirit, has set you free from the law of sin and death. Death has no more dominion over you. It cannot claim lordship. It cannot grip you like it once did. It cannot harass you and drag you down.

No condemnation does not mean "less condemnation" or "only sometimes condemnation." God's Word means what it says: *no* condemnation.

Because there is no condemnation, you are worthy to be in the very presence of the Almighty God. You are worthy because He is worthy, and you are in Him.

Because there is no condemnation, your sin no longer clings to you. It is gone, cast away forever, never to be returned.

Because there is no condemnation, you can look to the world and your neighbor and see what they need. You can help your neighbor, not because you must, but because you are free.

Jesus, help me to remember that there is no condemnation for those of us who are in You. Amen.

WEDNESDAY, LENT 5

Follow Me

Read Mark 8:31–9:1

And calling the crowd to Him with His disciples, He said to them, "If anyone would come after Me, let him deny himself and take up his cross and follow Me." (Mark 8:34)

Peter wanted to keep Jesus from the cross. He didn't want Jesus to take the way of sorrow. He wanted Jesus to be like the other disciples. But Jesus would have none of that. While the disciples might not have known it, Jesus' way did not end in death and destruction—not for Him or for us. His road is the *only* road that leads to eternal life.

Jesus calls out to the crowd, "If anyone would come after Me, let him deny himself and take up his cross and follow Me." Saying yes to Jesus means saying no to every idol, every false teacher, every temptation that will distract us from our focus on the cross and the life won for us in Jesus' death and resurrection.

This self-denial is not just depriving yourself of what you want. It is recognizing that you do not know what it means to follow Jesus. It means emptying yourself of pride, vanity, and everything that would draw you away from Christ and the path of life. This following, this discipleship, is a lifelong path renewed daily in your Baptism.

Lord, teach me the way to deny myself and follow You alone. In Jesus' name. Amen.

THURSDAY, LENT 5

So That You May Believe

Read John 11:1–16

Then Jesus told them plainly, "Lazarus has died, and for your sake I am glad that I was not there, so that you may believe. But let us go to him." (John 11:14–15)

This is a hard saying from Jesus. His friend Lazarus was sick to the point of death, but Jesus delayed going to him. Why? Why would He do that if it meant that Lazarus would die?

Sometimes, death strikes and we do not understand God's timing. It all seems so clear what God should do. How can He not see what seems so obvious to us? How can He mess this up so badly?

In our grief, we forget that every path we go down is one that Jesus has gone down before. He knows the way of eternal life. What may seem straightforward to us could be a snare of the devil, designed to entrap us and rip us away from the certain comfort that only comes from Him.

Jesus told His friends that He was glad He had not been there when Lazarus died, "so that you may believe." Everything is done so that you may believe in Him, and in believing in Him, so that you may have life. We may not understand why things happen as they do, but we know who is leading the way.

Jesus, give me faith to trust in You, especially when I do not understand Your ways. Amen.

FRIDAY, LENT 5

Resurrection

Read John 11:17–27

Jesus said to her, "I am the resurrection and the life. Whoever believes in Me, though he die, yet shall he live, and everyone who lives and believes in Me shall never die. Do you believe this?" (John 11:25–26)

In her piety, Mary tried to cover up her grief and pain and her doubts about who Jesus was. She wanted to look strong. She tried to look faithful, but underneath, Mary was afraid.

So are we. Death is such an unknown for us, and when we are in its grips, it is so hard to look to Jesus as the author and finisher of our faith.

Jesus' words, though, drew Mary right back to where she belonged. It is not that Jesus brings resurrection. He *is* the resurrection and the life. In Christ, there is no death, no sorrow, no pain. Because Christ has borne these, they now lie in the grave where Christ lay so many years ago.

Do you believe that in Christ you are raised from the dead? That is your Baptism into Him. And not only you but everyone who dies in Him now lives in Him.

That is why you do not need to be afraid . That is why you need not fear death and the grave.

> Teach me to live that I may dread
> The grave as little as my bed.
> Teach me to die that so I may
> **Rise glorious at the awe-full day**
> (*LSB* 883:3). Amen.

SATURDAY, LENT 5

Unbound

Read John 11:38–44

The man who had died came out, his hands and feet bound with linen strips, and his face wrapped with a cloth. Jesus said to them, "Unbind him, and let him go." (John 11:44)

The scene is almost funny, isn't it? The man came out of the grave, still bound up in the linen clothes. Death could not hold Lazarus, for the Lord of Life called him back from death.

There will come a time when the trappings of death will be just that—trappings that we no longer want or need. There will come a time when you will be raised from death, when Christ will call you out, and no earthly power will be able to keep you from Him.

That is our hope. Lazarus points us there. He points the way. The trappings that seem so somber, scary, and horrible will be nothing more than leftovers that are no longer needed.

That will be a scene. We get glimpses of the scene that is to come. The widow of Nain's son. Jairus's daughter. Lazarus, here in John 11. But none of them will compare to that great day when the graves will be emptied and we will be raised for all eternity.

The bonds that hold us now are nothing compared to the Word of the living Lord of Life.

Lord, free us from the bonds of sin and death, which still cling to us, and set us free in You. In Jesus' name. Amen.

Holy Week

PALM SUNDAY / PASSION SUNDAY

Every Knee

Read Philippians 2:5–11

At the name of Jesus every knee should bow, in heaven and on earth and under the earth, and every tongue confess that Jesus Christ is Lord, to the glory of God the Father. (Philippians 2:10–11)

Kneeling is a sign of humility and prayer. It is as if you are saying, "Here is my life; I lay it before you." Kneeling means you recognize the One who is greater than you are. It gives honor and respect to the greatness that existed before.

On the Last Day, every knee will bow. Some will bow in reverence and awe, for the baptized know who Jesus is. Some will bow because they cannot deny that He rose from the dead, even though they did not believe in Him. But on that Last Day, every knee will bow.

Every knee will bow because Jesus bowed low, bent under the weight of our sin and death. Jesus came down to earth, took on our flesh and blood, and set aside His power and might as the Son of God so that He could receive what we could not bear.

This week, we are on the final journey with Him to the cross and the tomb. Kneel before the Lord of Life, who gave up His life so that you might live.

Lord, teach us to kneel before You so that we may receive what only You can give. In Jesus' name. Amen.

MONDAY IN HOLY WEEK

How Much More?

Read Hebrews 9:11–15

For if the blood of goats and bulls . . . sanctify . . . how much more will the blood of Christ, who through the eternal Spirit offered Himself without blemish to God, purify our conscience from dead works to serve the living God. (Hebrews 9:13–14)

The blood of Christ is the only thing that can cleanse us from our sin. There is no such thing as a payment for sin apart from blood. The life is in the blood.

Apart from Christ, all our works, our very lives, are dead and useless. But with Him, we serve the living God. As we sing in "Now, My Tongue, the Mystery Telling":

Word made flesh, the bread He taketh,
By His word His flesh to be;
Wine His sacred blood He maketh,
Though the senses fail to see;
Faith alone the true heart waketh
To behold the mystery. (*LSB* 630:4)

This mystery cleanses us and makes our conscience clean, enabling us to serve not dead laws but a living God, who reigns forever.

Notice that our great High Priest offers Himself up before God as our one sacrifice for the sins of the world. Jesus is both our intercessor and High Priest, but He is also the very Lamb of God.

Heavenly Father, cleanse us by Your Holy Spirit so we may live forever in You. In Jesus' name. Amen.

TUESDAY IN HOLY WEEK

Foolishness

Read 1 Corinthians 1:18–25

For the foolishness of God is wiser than men, and the weakness of God is stronger than men. (1 Corinthians 1:25)

The word of the cross is foolishness to the world. It cannot understand a God who would give His own life for the sake of His wayward, wandering sheep. What kind of power is that? What God would ever act in such a way? As Paul wrote right before our text above, "For Jews demand signs and Greeks seek wisdom, but we preach Christ crucified, a stumbling block to Jews and folly to Gentiles" (1 Corinthians 1:22–23).

Christianity will always be a sideshow in the world, a way of life that makes no sense for those who cannot see past their so-called wisdom.

God does not argue us into faith. He does not convince with shows and power and might. He simply takes our sin into Himself and shows us the path that leads to eternal life in Him.

We look at the cross and death of Jesus, seeing through the gruesome picture, recognizing God's love in that great sacrifice. That is why the cross, an instrument of death, has become for us the very sign of life itself. If that makes us fools, then we are fools for Jesus.

Lord, teach us to be fools with You and to revel in Your weakness, which makes us strong. In Jesus' name. Amen.

WEDNESDAY IN HOLY WEEK

From Enemies to Friends

Read Romans 5:6–11

For if while we were enemies we were reconciled to God by the death of His Son, much more, now that we are reconciled, shall we be saved by His life. (Romans 5:10)

We often talk about death in connection with sin. But another of the images we get from the Scriptures is that we are enemies of God apart from His Son. An enemy is not passive. In death we are, well, dead. We don't do anything. But as an enemy, I actively work against another—in this case, God Himself.

But God, in His mercy, reconciles us to Himself in the death of His Son. Because of this, we are not the enemies of God but the friends of God. How hard it is to turn enemies into friends! This is why Jesus calls upon us to pray for our enemies (see Matthew 5:44). How can you hate someone you pray for?

Part of the Lenten season is about reconciliation with God and one another. Are there those you have hurt or harmed? Try reconciling with them. You were once God's enemy, and now He counts you as a "friend of God" like Abraham himself.

God longs to be reconciled to you in His Son, Jesus Christ. Cast away your enmity and embrace the love of God for us.

Lord, when I act as Your enemy, please forgive me and draw me back to You. In Jesus' name. Amen.

HOLY (MAUNDY) THURSDAY

Without

Read Hebrews 9:11–22

> Indeed, under the law almost everything is purified with blood, and without the shedding of blood there is no forgiveness of sins. (Hebrews 9:22)

Why blood? Why doesn't God just make a decree and erase sin without blood? Couldn't He do that?

The Law is the immutable, unchangeable will of God for us:

> The Law of God is good and wise
> And sets His will before our eyes,
> Shows us the way of righteousness,
> And dooms to death when we transgress.
> (*LSB* 579:1)

There is no such thing as a law without consequences. If we say something is a law but there are no consequences for breaking it, it is no longer a law but a suggestion. We would be making the law a lie.

The consequence of breaking God's Law is blood; it is our death. "The wages of sin is death," St. Paul writes in Romans 6:23.

So the author of Hebrews points us to the reality that the only way to pay the consequences, or the price, for sin is by blood, by death.

In the Old Testament, the sacrifice of the sin offering pointed to the one true and final sacrifice of Jesus Christ on the cross for our sins. When we receive His life-giving blood, we receive the payment for our sin, and new life is ours.

Lord, help me to know that the blood of God's Son, Jesus Christ, cleanses us from all sin. In His name. Amen.

GOOD FRIDAY

Our Confession

Read Hebrews 4:14–16; 5:7–9

Since then we have a great high priest who has passed through the heavens, Jesus, the Son of God, let us hold fast our confession. (Hebrews 4:14)

To confess something means to say the same thing about it that someone else has said. We confess a creed together, for example. We confess, or say the same thing, about God that God says about Himself. To confess, then, means to speak the truth that you have received.

We confess that Jesus Christ is our great High Priest. He is our intercessor, the mediator between God and us. By His death, He has removed anything that comes between us and God.

Our sins are no longer held against us. This means that our death now has no teeth, for Christ will raise us from the dead. This means that we will be with Him on the Last Day because Jesus passes into the heavens and sits at the Father's right hand. He will point to His hands and His side and say, "The price has been paid. They are my people."

The church has traditionally called today Good Friday. His death is good. His death is good because of His love for us. That is what we receive. That is what we confess.

Jesus, teach me to confess to all the world Your death and resurrection and everything You have done for us. Amen.

HOLY SATURDAY

Covered

Read 1 Peter 4:1–8

The end of all things is at hand; therefore be self-controlled and sober-minded for the sake of your prayers. Above all, keep loving one another earnestly, since love covers a multitude of sins. (1 Peter 4:7–8)

Jesus' resurrection ushers in the end of all things. We are in the Last Days even now. On this day, the eve of the Resurrection, our focus is on what the world misses and what we receive because of His resurrection from the dead.

The night before Easter is called the Easter Vigil. A vigil is a period of waiting, a time to gather together in anticipation of what is about to happen. It is a time of prayer, a time of repentance, and it is a time of waiting.

Because we are in these Last Days, in the Vigil before the end, we are also in a time of love. It is when we remember that because Jesus has paid the price for our sins and the sins of the whole world, we are free to love one another earnestly, as St. Peter reminds us.

Take this day to reconcile with those you have hurt or those who have hurt you. Love them, forgive their sins, cover them up, bury them, never to be seen again. That is what this day is about.

Rejoice! The day is at hand.

Jesus, teach us to forgive as You have forgiven us. Amen.

EASTER SUNDAY

Delivered

Read 1 Corinthians 15:1–11

For I delivered to you as of first importance what I also received: that Christ died for our sins in accordance with the Scriptures, that He was buried, that He was raised on the third day in accordance with the Scriptures. (1 Corinthians 15:3–4)

Jesus Christ is risen from the dead! Alleluia! Today is when everything Jesus has done for us all comes together. His incarnation, birth, Baptism, ministry, suffering, death, and resurrection all come into sharp focus, and we can now see what God was doing in Christ for us.

All of this means nothing unless it is delivered. So, Paul teaches us to pass on what we have received. Share the news of what God has done for us in Christ. This sharing is not cheesy. We aren't sharing a recipe from our favorite cookbook. This sharing means participating together in what God has done for us.

Are you ready for it? Are you prepared to be free of the sin and death that weigh you down? Are you prepared to share the sufferings of those around you so that they may share in the resurrection with you?

God has given us the most amazing gift in His Son, Jesus Christ. He changes everything. Alleluia!

> All glory to our Lord and God
> For love so deep, so high, so broad;
> The Trinity whom we adore
> Forever and forevermore (*LSB* 544:7). Amen.